We mobilize a movement of Christian women to pray and to proclaim the **Gospel of Jesus Christ.**

Check out our Linktree where you can find all the links in this issue!

FLOWCODE
PRIVACY.FLOWCODE.COM

We are prayer-filled communities who create environments of warm welcome and gracious hospitality, where relationships and leaders are developed so the Gospel can be shared.

Stonecroft

Dear Beloved Stonecroft Family,

Isn't it beautiful that God set in place a pattern and a rhythm for all things? We don't have to endure an endless frost of winter, nor the scorching sun of summer. By the time the seasons change, we are often ready for what is next and anticipating all the benefits the changes bring. What a good gift our Father lavishes on us to hide unique beauty inside transitions. I think he delights at our joy to discover, that while change is hard, there is more beauty and more life to embrace as we follow Him forward.

As a ministry, Stonecroft has walked through the seasons of 85+ years of change.

We have seen new initiatives, new leadership, new opportunities, new properties, new technology, and new ideas. And we acknowledge that every time we've stretched forward to lean in and change toward a new season, we've released something else in order to make space for it. Through it all, we see the hand of God at work. We must stop and notice - and celebrate - that some things remain unchanged.

We still exist to see women know and experience the love of God through Jesus Christ.

- We continue to choose to be uncomfortable in order to make others feel welcome.
- We have never stopped praying for God to move in our generations, and through us.
- We embrace learning, growing, and connecting in order to see God's Kingdom expand.

As this is our "Purpose" issue, it is noteworthy that our purpose as a ministry is anchored, unwavering, and resolute.

This issue represents the turning of a new season. Yes, a change in leadership, a new website, a new online store, a new featured Bible, and two new Outreach resources - with more on the horizon. You can be assured that even with all the new this season is bringing, Stonecroft will hold fast to who we have always been.

We are here for you, so you can be here for her.

Blessings and peace dear friends,

Suzy Shepherd

Your Stonecroft Staff Family

Stonecroft®

in this issue...

Every Ending

Dr. Naomi Cramer-Overton
CEO Emerita

23) "I do everything to spread the Good News and share in its blessings. 25) All athletes are disciplined in their training. They do it to win a prize that will fade away, but we do it for an eternal prize."
– 1 Corinthians 9:23, 25 New Living Translation (NLT)

When the U.S. men's and women's 4X100 meter relay teams won gold at the World Athletics Championships, every athlete got a prize. You see, in a relay race, every runner has their part - the first runner, those middle runners, and the exhilarating-to-watch final runner!

As I said yes to becoming Stonecroft's CEO in 2018 I knew my lap was a middle one. I celebrate that since then more than 10,000 women have started new life in Jesus! We've seen the dream of 1 million gospel proclamations become real. And more than 5,000 women have been sharing Jesus in daily life, especially helped through relational evangelism training.

Five years back, I accepted the role saying: "I am a change agent which means I will be useful for around five or so years. After that, I hope the ministry will be ready for a steadier building phase." I have glimpsed it coming for 15 months.

Now it's time for the next leg! On May 1, an athlete many already cheer on, our fabulous VP of Outreach Eliza Cortes Bast, takes her mark at the CEO-start line. Alongside her runs God's choice of a teammate in President/COO Elaine Watkins.

Will you join me in committing to pray for them?

And I thank God for how you have prayed for me. The Board has honored me to step into CEO Emerita shoes, introducing new people to Stonecroft, especially through my work with Every Woman's Bible.

I won't say goodbye, just "Let's keep loving people to Jesus." As CEO Emerita, I remain an advocate for and lover of this ministry and its people. With Christ building His Kingdom, the best is yet to come!

Brings a New Beginning

One of my favorite times to go to church is Christmas Eve. We have a tradition of ending in candlelight – each person passing their flame to their neighbor, until the whole place is illuminated. We sing Silent Night while the sanctuary is aglow, family and friends smiling as they light each other's wick.

Stories are like that. When I share my own story of how Jesus met my family, I tenderly share the spark of hope inside of me with whoever God has brought to me. I lean my candle towards them. And as I see them open their own hearts to my story, I can see a little flame ignite in them that slowly begins to glow.

Eliza Bast
CEO

I have had the joy over the last two years, of seeing women faithfully share their own rescue story. You all have kept your candle glowing – spreading the light of Jesus in large groups, patios, prisons, zoom calls, and living rooms. You have kept each other's fires burning as you've shared prayer requests, praise reports, victories, and challenges. This sisterhood is completely aglow with the love of Jesus for each other and for those who do not yet know Him.

For this next season, I am excited to find new ways for us to be ablaze with fresh stories! With new women who have just recently found their own spark. With women who have a candle but are waiting for a flame. With other Kingdom-minded partners, who are willing to share their flame. I see a future where the world is bathed in the amazing glow of women reconciled to God and the empowered, praying women who felt confident proclaiming the Good News of Jesus to them.

Thank you for allowing me to tend this flame with you!

My Story

A new tool to help you share your faith story

This tool was made to be a personal way to share the Gospel with others.
Scan the QR code to download this free resource! It will show you how to use it and includes a video as an example. We hope this will help you tell your story to others. Whether you use the actual printable with people or you use it as a tool to think through your story, it can help you be more confident as you share the ways Jesus has changed your life.

Try it & see if it really does help you tell your story!

1
It will print like this.

2
Simply follow the video instructions to fold and use.

The perfect fit for your pocket or wallet!

3

4

Scan for the Free Download Link

New FREE Tool to help you share your faith!

Introducing the
Every Woman's Bible

Janice Mayo Mathers

Why this Bible?

I've thought a lot about 'Why this Bible?,' because let's be honest - what woman in America needs another Bible? There is an embarrassing abundance of them in my own home!

So why am I buying this Bible, except to support Stonecroft?

One key reason: The Every Woman's Bible lives up to its name.

Every contributor is a woman - from the nationally recognized Bible scholars who wrote the commentary, to the mom in India telling how a passage helped her in her circumstances, to the single woman in Africa sharing why she identifies with a particular woman in the Bible.

All continents are represented - and I think 95 countries - women from every walk of life who've lived through every experience imaginable, sharing the applicability of the scripture to their circumstance.

It has a section called Middle Matter that deals with matters of interest to today's woman. For example, one subtitle is: Ten Scriptures Women Love to Hate, which takes on those Bible verses women tend to have issues with and shows the meaning of that scripture in its complete context.

As a woman, I personally want this Bible.

And although I've already bought both my nieces Bibles years ago, I can't wait to put this one in their hands so they can hear the voices of women around the world who have found the precious ancient words of God applicable to them today. Maybe it will help them discover its applicability to themselves. I can't wait to put it into my granddaughter's hands, growing up in a culture desperately searching for God in the opposite direction of where He will be found.

I can't wait to put it into my friend's hand who's walked away from God, and when I do, I will page-mark the woman's story that I know she will relate to. It is the distinct feminine focus of the sidebars that I think will be the magnet that keeps her turning the pages, and as she does so, reading snatches of the word of God on those pages that is unchanged and powerful, sharper than any two-edged sword - and those snatches will become paragraphs and then pages as it transforms her life and introduces her to her life's purpose.

Janice Mayo Mathers is the author of several books and has been a columnist with Today's Christian Women an Virtue magazines. A conference and retreat, Janice also serves as Chairwoman of the Board of Directors for Stonecroft. She is the author of popular Stonecroft studies *Ephesians* and *Loving Your Neighbor* as well. She lives in Bend, Oregon, where she and her husband, Steve, operate a four-generation well-drilling business.

EVERY WOMAN'S BIBLE

Introducing Stonecroft's new featured Bible, the Every Woman's Bible. Featuring notes, commentary, and application by women, for women, this Bible is a relevant and timely tool to reach further than ever. Dr. Naomi Cramer Overton, CEO Emerita of Stonecroft Ministries, is the General Editor of the Every Woman's Bible, with many of Stonecroft's volunteers and leaders also having contributed to the supplemental content.

Every Woman's Bible doesn't shy away from the questions women ask. In these pages, active and impactful women of yesterday and today share age-old truths with modern relevance. Contributions from more than 100 women around the world - from every continent - explore the heartfelt needs, gritty challenges, and uncommon faithfulness of women of the Bible, throughout history, and today. Serious study and deep reflection will help you clarify your calling through personal stories, insights, inspiration, and study notes that dig into personal needs during your Bible reading - all created by women, for women.

Order The Every Woman's Bible here

Extraordinary Leadership
in Unexpected Places

Eddie Baiseri

Have you ever thought about what it will be like in Heaven? I sometimes imagine meeting the people we read about in scripture. Naturally, my number one person to meet is Christ, that goes without saying, but I am also looking forward to meeting others who made the Bible come to life for me. I would like to meet Peter and ask him what it was like to walk on water and then there's Noah, Jonah, Paul and Silas, Moses and Mary, and my goodness the list goes on and on! But the person I am really excited to meet is Ruth. When I read her story I am so encouraged by her work ethic, humility, and godly character. She's an extraordinary leader.

Leaders are COMMITTED

The story of Ruth is told in a tiny book bearing her name in the Old Testament. Ruth was an outsider who found herself in a tough situation when at a young age her husband died, leaving her destitute and an unprotected widow. Ruth faced the decision whether to move with her mother-in-law or to go back to her own mother's home. Ruth fully committed her life to the one true God and chose to go with her mother-in-law and leave everything she knew behind. I like commitment - and I suppose you do as well - most of all, God honors commitment and He honored and favored Ruth when she declared her unwavering devotion to Him. She told Naomi, her mother-in-law, *"Wherever you go, I will go, wherever you live, I will live. Your people will be my people and your God will be my God." (Ruth 1:16)*

Leaders turn COMPASSION INTO ACTION

Everyone is struggling - some just hide it better than others. You don't have to look far to find someone who needs a word of encouragement, a smile or a prayer. When Naomi, Ruth's mother-in-law, was having a very difficult time she became convinced that the Lord was punishing her because in a short period of time her husband and both of her sons had died. In spite of Naomi's bitterness, Ruth displayed great compassion and her care turned into action. Ruth took the initiative to do what she could to support Naomi in her time of need. May we all willingly offer our gifts and talents to be a blessing. Ruth told Naomi of her plan, "Let me go into the harvest fields to pick up the stalks of grain..." (Ruth 2:2)

Everyone is struggling

some just hide it better than others.

-Eddie Baiseri

Leaders recognize the CONTRIBUTION OF OTHERS

Nothing is more commendable than gratitude. Ruth was quick to express her thankfulness to Boaz who had allowed her to gather grain in his fields. Ruth recognized his kindness and with a humble heart she asked, *"What have I done to deserve such kindness?" (Ruth 2:10)*

Boaz, who is a picture of Christ, provided protection and provision for Ruth, just as Christ does for us. As women who are grateful for grace and mercy we cry out to Christ, "Who am I Lord that you care for me?" and He answers, "I have loved you with an everlasting love." From the story of Ruth I learned that true leaders don't always come in nicely wrapped packages. We aren't all that different than Ruth and Naomi were in their day. We can find ourselves overworked and exhausted. We juggle children and budgets, and lives that are stretched to the limit. Some are hurting from wounds that time has yet to heal. Possibly you are strong and able to reach across the aisle to help someone in need, we all have seasons, we all need Jesus. One of my favorite scriptures in the entire Bible is found in a blessing that Boaz prayed over Ruth. I hope you'll personalize this blessing and tuck it deeply within your heart.

"May the Lord, the God of Israel, under whose wings you have come to take refuge, reward you fully for what you have done." (Ruth 2:12)

When I get to heaven I hope to tell Ruth, "Thank you, you inspired me to courageously go, to humbly serve and to remember to be thankful... in other words, to strive to be extraordinary!"

Eddie Baiseri, passionate teacher, speaker and author, sharing the timeless message of God's amazing love. She has 2 sons and is "Honey" to 2 grandkids. She loves to wear stretchy pants, grow zinnias and read.

Stonecroft®

Some of our...

Stonecroft®

amazing volunteers!

The Purpose Issue | Pg 19

Join us for the

State of the Ministry Call

Make sure you register by following the QR code on the next page and mark your calendar

for this special event!

You'll hear all the wonderful ways we see God at work through the women of Stonecroft, and fresh vision for all that is yet to come.

This is an exciting season in the life of this ministry, and we want you to be part of it!

Register Today!

Join us for the

State of the Ministry Call

4/30/24

State of the Ministry Call

REGISTER NOW!

3:30 Alaska | 4:30 Pacific | 5:30 MTN | 6:30 pm CST | 7:30 EST

Here for you

so you can be

Here for Her

Stonecroft

We are followers of Jesus, a community of believing women, an army passionately pursuing others with the love of God.

We refuse to be distracted by denomination, politics or comparison. We do things that often seem crazy to the world in order to reach those dying to know hope.

We get uncomfortable, give up our seats, pray on our knees, invite with abandon, scan crowds for the lost, share what we have, and make space so that everyone is welcome.

We know that it is God who moves hearts, but that he loves to use willing women in His work. We find our deepest purpose, our greatest joy, and our most sincere hope in wild, reckless obedience to His call.

We are a mix of experiences and identities: wives, mothers, aunts, grandmothers, partners, leaders, encouragers, messengers, professionals. We are behind-the-scenes and right-out-front.

We are friends. We are sisters. We are co-laborers.

Connect with us!

FACEBOOK

INSTAGRAM

$128,970 RAISED

THANK YOU

THE STORY GOES on through YOU.

WHO IS Stonecroft?

85+ years

100,000+ women

15,000+ volunteers

Cream Cheese
CUPCAKES

Recipe found in the 1978 edition of the Stonecroft Family Cookbook.

Ingredients

2- 8 oz Pakgs. Cream Cheese
2 Eggs
3/4 c Sugar
1 Tbs. Vanilla
Vanilla wafers
Favorite pie filling (apple, cherry, blueberry, etc.)

Directions

Combine cream cheese and sugar. Add eggs and vanilla. Mix well. Place 1 wafer in the bottom of a cupcake liner. Fill each cupcake liner 1/2 full with cheese filling and bake at 350 degrees for 15 minutes. Cool and top with any pie filling. One can of pie filling will top 12 cupcakes. Serves 24. (For 12 cupcakes, cut recipe in 1/2 using a heaping 1/4 c. sugar in place of 3/4 cup.)

Anne has been working with Stonecroft home office for a year and has a passion for food and community. She believes cooking for people is a fun way for God to open the door for conversation. Isaiah 58:7

"*Our circumstances don't define our purpose*"

Have you ever woken up and wondered, "What is my purpose?"

If you're not finding meaning in buying groceries, doing laundry, and paying bills, you're not alone. The good news is that you were designed for rich relationships with God and others. You were designed for a unique purpose — that only you can do! And even though you might feel ordinary, you were made to fulfill an extraordinary purpose.

Prepare to laugh, make new friends, and discover a fresh anticipation for life. In *Ordinary People. Extraordinary Purpose.™*, you will:
• **Dive into fun activities**
• **Discuss spiritual topics at your level of comfort and curiosity**
• **Go deep — with others and on retreats you can do on your own**

You'll see what purpose looks like in the lives of people in the Bible and easily find Scripture references with verses noted to pages in Tyndale's Every Woman's Bible and Abundant Life Bible. In the New Testament books of Matthew, Mark, Luke, and John you'll encounter people whose lives may feel something like your own. And as you notice the ways that they used their influence, you'll be equipped by God to exercise your own. God has created you for this.

We all do daily life that can feel very ordinary. But we can live extra-ordinary — while fulfilling our purpose — today. This fun experience and journey through the Gospels belongs to the Ordinary People. Extraordinary Purpose.™ series brought to you by Stonecroft — a group of ordinary people living with extraordinary purpose by connecting with God, each other, and our communities. Since 1938, Stonecroft has created opportunities for hundreds of thousands to explore the Bible together in community in more than forty nations. Ordinary People. Extraordinary Purpose.™ is accompanied by videos and a Leader's Guide, available at shop.stonecroft.org.

The many forms of
Mothering

Suzy Shepherd

The "motherhood" I've known has included bonus kids, step kids, bio kids, adopted grands, and kids in my school classrooms. All of them are unique in their own way, with the fingerprints of their Maker all over their lives in different forms. I've learned through all of them that whether they are a child I've influenced or a child I've raised, there's nothing like seeing them follow Jesus.

Lately women baking bread from a sourdough starter have inspired me. I loved the idea of this but had no idea how to start a starter! My family has heard me wonder about the idea.

One day my son John came in the door with a grin and an envelope.

He found a company that sells a starter which is over 100 years old, and even has a name - Sophia! The starter comes from San Francisco and he ordered the packet and instructions for me.

His gift was awesome, but the best part was seeing my grown son in a brand-new way. He had heard, took note of, and went to the trouble of honoring a desire.

I used to imagine the best part of parenting would be when they were snuggly, chunky-legged babies. That was a wonderful part of parenting (exhausting, but wonderful) but it just kept getting better.

"Whether they're a child you've influenced or a child you've raised, there are few gifts as sweet as seeing one you love follow Jesus."

Suzy Shepherd

They are young adults now and I am now delighted to enjoy their great conversations, big ideas, new adventures, and deep laughs. I no longer lift them up or tuck them in, instead I look up to them as they greet me with their bear hugs. From time to time, they still come and lay on top of the covers beside me to talk about something they need to process. I still get to pray over them, but now it's as they go for job interviews or first dates instead of out the door for school in the morning.

Most of all, I love to hear their prayers and their developing perspectives on faith. They call to mind the verse, "I have no greater joy than to see my children walking in the truth."

This Mother's Day, I encourage you to make a list of those you've influenced, praying for them and giving thanks for the evidence you see of God's love for them.

No matter how or whom you've mothered,
your influence matters.

Suzy Shepherd is an entrepreneur, speaker, author, and nonprofit leader. She currently serves as Vice President of Growth at Stonecroft. She loves helping others find their calling and dare to follow God in it. She lives in downtown Tyler, Texas with her 3 sons, ages 14-22, and their gigantic, very sweet dog Waylon. She also loves getting to be close with her bonus daughters, and being "Ewwy" to two grandsons.

Don't forget to check out our

New Merch!

shop.stonecroft.org

How God's Love *Transformed* My Life.

Beth Carriere

I grew up in a family very involved in church in southeast Louisiana. My dad was a deacon and my mom taught Sunday school, so we were in church every time the doors were open, and sometimes even when they were closed. I've known about God for as long as I can remember, but I haven't always understood how much He knows and loves me.

My father was a hard man, not very emotional, and he had a lot of rules and expectations. As a result, I started to see God as someone who expected more from me than what I could give. So I quit trying. I had so much anger, confusion, and bitterness inside me that I didn't know how to handle it, so I took it out on myself. At 12, I started a cycle of self-abuse that kept me in and out of hospitals and institutions for the next several years. By age 17, I was searching everywhere for a way to fill the void.

Over the next few years I began to look for love in relationships with men, while also falling into other traps like heavy drinking, smoking, and drugs. At age 19, I met a man I thought would change my life. He promised me a life where we could make our own rules so, naively, I married him.

Not long after our wedding I started to see who he really was - a liar who was easily angered, an unfaithful partner who broke the covenant of our marriage, and a narcissistic abuser who never took responsibility for his actions but took his anger out on me instead. I knew what kind of person he was, but I told myself that I couldn't find anyone better. I'd made way too many mistakes, so no one else could ever love me.

After two years of marriage I couldn't take the abuse anymore so I gathered up the courage to leave. But I was broken, carrying so much heaviness and guilt inside me. I hated myself and needed someone else to love me, someone to show me that I was worth it. So before my divorce was even filed, I was already dating someone new. This new man said all the right things, but made promises he couldn't keep - like the promise to stay sober. I found myself right back in the cycle of abuse. A year and a half later, we had a child. From that moment, I knew I had to break the cycle for my son, so we left.

Yet even through the storms, I knew God was calling me to

something more.

Beth Carriere

I wish I could say this is where I turned my life around. Unfortunately there were many more bad choices that came over the next few years. There were many wrong turns, shattered relationships, and struggles that came from being a single mom. Yet even through the storms, I knew God was calling me to something more.

In June of 2015, I lost someone I loved, a close friend who always encouraged me to use my gifts and pursue a life of ministry. The loss of this friend shattered me, but it also put my life into perspective. One night I cried out to God in my living room, pouring out all the words I'd held in for so long.

"I'm so sorry. I know this isn't what you wanted for me. I really messed up. I can't live like this anymore."

In that moment, I fully surrendered my life back to God and committed to never go back to that life again.

Since that night, I've watched God transform every single area of my life - my desires, my relationships, my finances, my family. I've seen him provide groceries from a friend who didn't know we were hungry, rent money from strangers who didn't know we were struggling, other bills or random expenses that I could've never paid on my own… and so much more.

I've seen him break the cycle of abuse and heal the damaged pieces of my heart. I've seen him realign my thoughts and plans to the ones he has for me, and watched as he used my testimony to work in the lives of others around me. God has seen every single detail of my messy life, yet he pours out his kindness and mercy to me anyway. It took me awhile, but now I understand - the love of God, my Father, my Provider, my Savior, my Friend - is the only love that can take the brokenness and make it whole.

Beth Carriere leads a nonprofit cottage bakery that provides free birthday cakes to the children of single parents in her community. She is also a mom, writer, and music lover, who has a heart to see others transformed by the love of God.

The
Stonecroft Store

We are excited to introduce The Stonecroft Store, a hub for all your favorite Stonecroft studies! Immerse yourself in an unparalleled experience. Our online store is a product of passion, designed meticulously to offer you top-notch products. We are grateful to have you on this journey with us! Shipping is included in every order, guaranteeing a seamless checkout process.

If you have any questions about our products, don't hesitate to contact Connie at orders@stonecroft.org. She will be happy to help you find the information you seek.

Featuring

- The Every Woman's Bible
- Small Group Experience
- Outreach Resources
- Stonecroft Classics

Meet Connie
Our Fulfillment Specialist

We are happy to introduce Connie Conaway as our Fulfillment Specialist. She is "Nonnie" to two precious grandchildren. She loves to thrift and turned her side business into e-commerce and then a thriving boutique. She now serves Stonecroft by fulfilling your products and orders placed on the store. Connie is here for you so you can be *here for her!*

The Pursuit of Purpose

Nichole Masters-Henry is a passionate advocate who uses her own life experiences to inspire and encourage others to overcome adversities. She is mom to Eli, 18 and makes her home in East Texas. She is an ordained minister and a nonprofit leader. Nichole has dedicated her life to serving others and with her infectious smile, caring demeanor, and generous heart she leaves an indelible imprint on the lives of those she encounters.

Purpose. This simple 7-letter word is tossed around women's bible study groups, Christian conferences, women's day luncheons, and private conversations between friends as an elusive, mythical idea that only a few are fortunate to stumble upon.

Discovering one's purpose has become the primary focus for many believers. There are countless devotions, books, seminars, conferences, and women's brunches promising to answer the questions we all ask: What is my purpose? What do I do next? What am I supposed to be doing with my life? We dive in with our pens and journals hoping to get the mysterious key that will unlock the answers that will change our lives, awaken our destiny, and catapult us into our purpose-filled future. Alas, we close the books, logout of the virtual seminars, and leave the conferences encouraged and energized - feeling good about moving forward. However, weeks later we are back to where we began asking "what am I supposed to be doing?" The sense of emptiness, the longing for more seems to never end.

Dear friends, I believe we've over complicated the process of finding purpose. I hope after reading this today you will have questions answered, doubts erased, and an increased understanding of how to pursue your God-given purpose.

As a minister I've heard those questions listed above many times from women in our congregation, friends, and strangers. In my early years I'd recite the same steps, which haven't changed much over the decades I've served. What has changed is my initial response. After years of walking this out I've realized the hang up, what keeps so many asking this question isn't about the process but the starting point. Now when asked my response is, "How is your walk with Christ?" Often when we are feeling unsure of what's next, unfulfilled, unproductive, a yearning for more what really is missing or depleted is our connection with the Father. So, before we jump into it today I'd like to ask you a few questions:

How is your walk with the Father?

How is your prayer life? How often do you get to pray?

Do you pray and allow time to listen?

How often do you have quiet, reflective time? This is time beyond the 15-minute morning devotional and bed-time popcorn prayer.

How often do you read/listen to the Holy Scriptures?

Do you meditate on HIS word?

In Luke chapter 10 verses 38-42 we read the story of two sisters, Mary and Martha, and their encounter with Jesus. One sister, Martha, is busy preparing for the visit with Jesus. I imagine frantically cleaning, preparing the meal, ensuring everything is just right because Jesus is coming. Upon his arrival she continues her work, diligently serving so everything is perfect for the Master. However, Mary has chosen a different response. She isn't scurrying around making the home perfect, instead she tends to Him, she sits at His feet and listens. Martha, bothered by her sister's inattention to the work needing to be done, complains to Jesus and His response is, "You are worried and upset about many things, but few things are needed—or indeed only one. Mary has chosen what is better, and it will not be taken away from her."

We most note that Christ *doesn't* say that Martha is wrong for her desire and dedication to serving but what He does say is between the two of them Mary has made the better choice and that is to focus on Him.

In our pursuit of purpose, fulfillment, and destiny we can get so caught up in the business of doing that we forget why, or better yet, to whom our service is unto. Like Martha the primary focus is getting it done and getting it right - again there's nothing wrong with that. **The problem arises when the service, the promise, the purpose, becomes priority over our ultimate call - and that's to Christ.**

That *one thing* that is needed is referenced in Psalm 27:4 "One thing I ask from the Lord, this only do I seek: that I may dwell in the house of the Lord all the days of my life, to gaze on the beauty of the Lord and to seek him in his temple."

When was the last time seeking His face was your priority?

Once you've reprioritized
Christ in your life, identifying
your purpose will come.

Nichole Masters-Henry

Once you've reprioritized Christ in your life identifying your purpose will come. Here are short tips on how to pursue with Christ at the center.

1. Prayerful Pursuit

Our purpose begins with **prayerful pursuit.** Like Jeremiah, we were formed by God's hands, intricately designed for a divine purpose. In Jeremiah 1:4-5, God declares, "Before I formed you in the womb, I knew you; before you were born, I sanctified you." Our purpose is not happenstance; it's a deliberate creation. Seek God's face in prayer, for it is there that He whispers His plans into our hearts.

2. Passionate Obedience

When he instructs, move in obedience. Often, we hesitate - like Jeremiah - to embrace our purpose. Fear of inadequacy and comfort zones hold us back. But God calls us to **passionate obedience**. He equips those He calls. Just as He assured Jeremiah, "I am with you," He promises to be our companion on this purposeful journey. Step out in faith, even when it feels uncomfortable. Our purpose lies beyond the familiar shores.

3. Persevering Commitment

Purpose isn't a fleeting emotion; it's a **persevering commitment.** God's Word fuels our purpose. As we study Scripture, we hear His voice. Like a blacksmith shaping iron, God molds us through His Word. We may stumble, but He steadies our steps. Our purpose isn't a solo endeavor; it's a partnership with the Almighty. Cry out to Him, seek His guidance, and allow Him to work through you.

Dear sisters, your purpose isn't elusive - it's etched in eternity. **Prayerful pursuit, passionate obedience,** and **persevering commitment** will unveil it. As you walk this path, remember: God gives purpose, but you must know Him to find yours. Invite Jesus Christ into your heart today, and let His purpose flow through your life like a mighty river.

Check out our

New Website!

stonecroft.org

Stonecroft Leader Site

Are you already leading a Stonecroft Outreach?
If so, click the link below to take you to our volunteer site.

If you're interested in learning more about how to lead an outreach in your local community, click below.

ENTER THE LEADER PORTAL

Stonecroft is here for you, so you can be

Here for Her

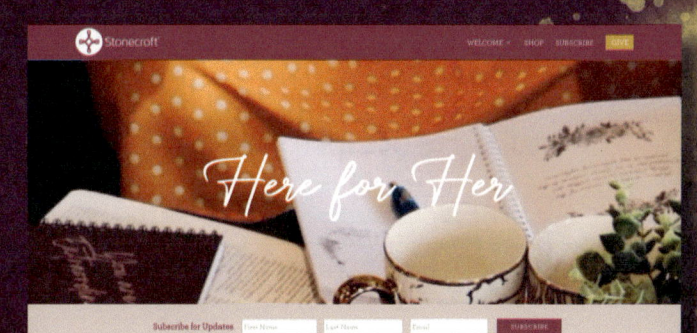

Here for Her

Subscribe for Updates

We are on a mission to **mobilize** a **movement** of Christian women to **pray** and **proclaim** the *Gospel of Jesus Christ*.

Here for
Her

If you're looking for a community of women committed to share the Gospel, Stonecroft is the place for you. Like so many women before you have said,

"I have found my people!"

The Purpose Issue | Pg 45

Where to start *with Stonecroft*

At Stonecroft, we believe that **Relational Evangelism training** is a basic need for Christian women who wish to confidently pray for people, listen to others' stories, and tell the story of what Jesus has done for them. Stonecroft's Bootcamp is a great place to begin.

Bootcamp is an introductory version of our 4-week Relational Evangelism course. By attending Bootcamp, you'll learn three key essentials that help you continue to be more and more aware of opportunities to share your faith every day, everywhere God takes you.

The **Foundations for Sharing Your Faith** study guide is now available through the Stonecroft Store. The study guide includes the essentials covered in Bootcamp and more. It's beneficial for both Bootcamp and the 4-week course participants. Begin this journey by registering to attend an upcoming Bootcamp by visiting the link on the next page!

Dale Shelton has been with Stonecroft for 7 years and is currently serving as the Stonecroft Community Manager. Her greatest joys include family competitions (especially with her nieces and nephews) - and she's passionate about using her gifts to help unlock the gifts and talents of those around her.

Testimonial

"I have signed up and attended five different Foundations workshops. Through Zoom I have met women from all over the country who struggle (like me) with how to start up a 'faith conversation' with a family member, friend or complete stranger."

Carolyn Griffith

Register to attend:

my.stonecroft.org/relational-evangelism-bootcamp/

Order copies for your group at:

shop.stonecroft.org/product/foundations-for-sharing-your-faith/

THE **JOY** OF
Generosity

Heidi Farinas

On the wall beside my desk there is a little note card with my life verse on it. *"The man answered, 'You must love the Lord your God with all your heart, all your soul, all your strength, and all your mind.' And, 'Love your neighbor as yourself.' "*
-Luke 10:27 NLT

Many years ago, when I became a Christian, I was asking all of the questions that many of us ask. What is my purpose on earth? What did God create me uniquely to do? Now that I know who I am and that I am saved by the grace and mercy of God, how do I live that out? Then this verse, that so many of us read every day, spelled it out in black and white for me. What am I to do? Love and worship God. And love my neighbor as myself.

Relationship is so important to God, so important that He invites us into the work that He does and commands us to be in relationship with others. Because He knows how badly we need the love, kindness, and support of each other.

He knows the power of relationships to fulfill His purposes on earth. Whether the purpose is to invite someone to know Jesus, offer a volunteer opportunity, or to ask someone to give financially, relationships are the most important tools we have.

When we journey through life with someone, learning their story, their unique passions which God has predestined for them before the foundations of the earth, we must pray with them, watch God stretch them, and love them for the amazing person they are, that is when we are able to understand the ways that God is calling them.

Opportunities are from God. We just match people to opportunities, support them along the way, and watch Him work. He provides abundantly for this work and calls each of us uniquely.

My heart is for every woman to know the lifesaving truth of the Gospel.

Over 30 years ago, I was a military wife who was 12 hours from home and was invited to church by my friends. I wasn't seeking a church home or Jesus; I just wanted a place to belong. That need for relationship and those women were the catalyst for a life changed.

Every day I am blessed to build relationships, care for His servants, offer opportunities to build His kingdom, and to report back on the good work that He is doing. I am burdened to love God's people; for them to know Him, to grow in Him, and to steward His resources responsibly knowing that they are given for the glory of God.

Hopefully when I meet you, I will have the chance to inspire you with stories of Stonecroft's impactful work, prayers answered, and lives changed, encircle you with prayer, love, and support. And then equip you to reach one more.

> " My heart is for every woman to know the lifesaving *truth of the Gospel.* "

Heidi Farinas

Meet Heidi Farinas
Our Donor Engagement Director

Heidi and her husband, Marc, have two adult children, Lily and Bella, who live in Florida and Tennessee. Now empty nesters, they love living in East Tennessee. Much of their free time is enjoyed outdoors in God's creation and playing pickleball.

God called Heidi to Stonecroft after many years of serving givers in Christian ministries. She has a Political Science degree from Old Dominion University and has served at Precept Ministries, pregnancy centers, churches, and in children's social services. Caring for givers and leading teams to discover the abundant opportunities God has for them in His Kingdom, is her life purpose. It is a great joy for her to partner with givers to grow the kingdom of God, and she is full of gratitude that God allows her to serve His people.

Having been saved as an adult and a former military wife, she has a heart for mobilizing generations of women to pray and proclaim the gospel of Jesus Christ. Heidi and her husband, Marc, love spending time in nature, boating, hiking, leading youth ministry and playing pickle ball. Every day she spends caring for His people and living in the beautiful state of Tennessee is a blessing.

Stonecroft MILITARY TEAM

STORIES FROM *the Front Line*

Do you know there is a special Stonecroft team who ministers to military families on bases across the country?

In February, they held a special Valentine outreach for children of military families. With 38 in attendance, children memorized verses and used the Valentine downloadable from the last magazine. This is the Good News Club at FE Warren Freedom Elementary School.

Their work goes far beyond Valentine's Day.

Here's how they took the Gospel to these special families in 2023:

- **They hosted 124 calls**
- **12 Saturdays of Prayer**
- **7 Prayer Walks**
- **20 Outreaches**
- **23 Speaking Engagements...**
- **and best of all,**

65 DECISIONS FOR CHRIST!

We praise God for the dedicated work of the Stonecroft Military team.
May God continue to richly bless the work of your heart and hands!

Work in Progress

Designed for
Today's Christian

Excerpt from May 1981 edition of "Progress"

Extraordinary

By Judy McGinnis

"How can I be sure there is a God?" was my question to the pastor as a teenager. The answer to that question could have been a turning point in my life, but all the pastor said was to look at the trees, the birds, the sky - that nature itself proved God's existence.

I found no comfort in such proof. For one thing, scientist claimed that the things of nature could be explained by natural causes. But more to the point, a God who created nature was not necessarily a God who cared about individuals, who cared about me.

As a child I was very interested in God. Born in Honolulu where my father was stationed in the service, we spent most of my childhood in El Paso, Texas. My parents reared my younger brother, Bob, and me with good Christian morals. Although they were of different faiths and had agreed to not influence our decisions about religion, they took us to church when we were small and never discouraged us from going by ourselves as we got older.

Early I decided to try to please God by being good. After hearing a sermon, I'd vow to be good the whole next week and NOT fight with my brother nor say anything mean to my parent. But I failed every time. Always there were the haunting questions: "How can I be sure there is a God?" and "What is the purpose of life?"

Despite the questioning, I enjoyed my teen years and was voted "the girl with the best personality" by my senior class. During my last two years of high school I dated Dale McGinnis, an airman stationed in El Paso. Mac and I were married soon after my graduation.

We moved to Ohio, Mac's home state, when he was discharged from the Air Force two years later. Basically, I was happy in my new home with everything I had always wanted, a nice husband, a family, a house of my own. There were no uppers, no downers; I was just a plain, ordinary person with a constant searching, a wondering about God.

When people said things about God giving them strength when they were in trouble, I just knew they were using the idea of God as an escape because they couldn't cope otherwise. God would not be a cop-out for me.

Still, I can remember being pregnant with Julie, my second child, and standing over Allen's crib with tears running down my cheeks, just wondering why I was having these kids. If there was no God, there was no meaning to my life, or to theirs. They would just die and rot in the ground.

I was miserable and my questions about God and about purpose for living became stronger all the time. Even so, it was not possible to express my doubts to anyone. Surely they would be shocked to find that a nice, normal person like me didn't believe in God!

At that time some new neighbors Donna and Judd Scott, moved in next door. They were very religious, and even though their family life was hectic, they seemed so calm about everything that it made me curious.

Fearful of asking Donna my questions about God, I tried to jab at her to upset her, just to see how she would react. Nothing seem to phase Donna, and she never said anything offensive to me. She was always friendly and soon invited me to go to a Christian women's club luncheon.

The first time Donna asked, I was afraid, but she was going to pay my way! My only memory from that luncheon is that everyone was very, very friendly.

Over the next four years Donna never gave up; she asked me to the luncheon every month. Sometimes I'd find an excuse not to go - pretend to be sick or busy - but other times I went. Every time, as the speaker talked about receiving Christ I would think "Maybe that's the reason. Some people seem to have purpose in their lives that I want."

But this all remained meaningless to me until I became convinced that God was real, that He cared for me and had purpose for my life.

Finally, one day in January 1974, after four years of luncheons, a dentist's wife spoke about her struggle with the same words that plagued me. "What is the purpose to life?" she had wondered. "What is going to happen to my children?" Her life had been similar to mine; there were no tragedies, but she experienced a deep in longing for peace and purpose.

All through her talk, I kept thinking, "That lady was sent here just for me." After the luncheon, I went up to her and told her my uncertainties. How could there be a God with all the terrible things that were happening?

She looked at me and said, "The trouble with you, Judy, is that you want all of the answers first, and then you'll decide whether or not you'll become a Christian. But God wants you just as you are and then He'll teach you." Then she asked, "Would you like to pray now?"

In a panic, I said, "No! I'm not ready for that yet."

Walking to my car with tears streaming down my face, I couldn't stand another moment of indecision. So there in my own car, driving, I prayed, "God, I don't know if you're there or not. I just know I can't live like this anymore. If you're there, I'm yours."

From that point on there were no doubts that God was there. I was finally willing to learn, and Donna encouraged me to attend a Bible-teaching church and a woman's Bible study group. Beginning to understand Bible verses that had been meaningless to me before, I became aware of all that Christ had done for me.

For instance, I soon realized that Romans 3:23 - "For all have and come short of the glory of God..." included me. All my earlier attempts to be a good person weren't enough to cover the wrong that I had also done. No matter how good I managed to be, God still wasn't pleased because I was a sinner. For the first time, I also discovered that I was more than an impersonal part of creation. My love for my own children helped me understand what it meant for God to give up His Son, Jesus, to die for sinful people. That meant me!

Romans 6:23 became very personal then. "For the wages of sin is death; but the gift of God is eternal life through Jesus Christ, our Lord." God was offering me eternal life through his son, Jesus Christ. How could I not accept his gift?

After years of searching for a purpose in life, that purpose was found in the words of Jesus: "I am the way, the truth, and the life: no man come unto the father but by me." (John 14:6) Suddenly, it was clear that long before I had asked the questions, Christ had given the answer - the only logical answer to all my needs.

The change in my life - the disappearance of those deep longings that had haunted me - was just incredible once I accepted Christ as my Savior. With a newfound purpose for living, the everyday things became joyful. It was almost like looking at the world in a new way, as if I had never seen it before.

At first, my husband didn't understand. When I told Mac of my experience with Christ, he thought it was just a fad and he waited for it to wear off. I said very little to him about my new faith, afraid of turning him away.

Before long, though, at the children's insistence, Daddy started coming to church with us. Just one year after my conversion, Mac, too, accepted the Lord.

I thrived on Christian Fellowship and became active in my church and in Christian Women's Club. I served as Special Feature Chairman in 1975, the year after I came to Christ; then became Chairman of Christian Women's Club during 1976 and 1977, and currently am Chairman.

Our children have both accepted Christ, too - Allen when he was six and Julie three years later. It's wonderful having a Christian family.

It's strange sharing a story of how Christ worked in my life because I was just a plain, ordinary person. As far as anyone could tell, I didn't have any real problems. But God knew my secret longings.

I'm sure now that there is a God, for he took the ordinary and made it extraordinary through my new life in Christ.

Carolyn Griffith

The story goes on...

through you.

My mother invited me to my first Stonecroft Luncheon in 1985. I attended with her a few times and enjoyed it but then got busy raising a family and juggling our hectic Marine Corps life with my husband deploying every few years, so it was easier to drop out. My mother continued to ask, and I continued to say, "no" until the time was right.

In 1995 I was asked to become the Vice Chair for the Santa Ana - Tustin CWC. Within a year I was asked to be Chairman. Over the years I have served every position except Nursery Chair. I have served as Chairman and Area Rep in 3 different clubs in Orange County.

I love everything Stonecroft has to offer women, whether they are serving in a Leadership role or just attending a luncheon or one of our amazing Bible Studies. I especially love the "Relational Evangelism" classes offered online. I have signed up and attended five different RE workshops. Through Zoom I have met women from all over the country who struggle (like me) with how to start up a "faith conversation" with a family member, friend or complete stranger. I have been amazed how God has used the tools I've been given through these classes to bolden my heart to be a blessing, be a friend, encourage someone, witness, and pray for people. I encourage every woman to register for the free Relational Evangelism Workshop if you'd like to experience "Intentional Faith Conversations" and make a difference in someone's eternity.

**Scan here
to share
your story!**

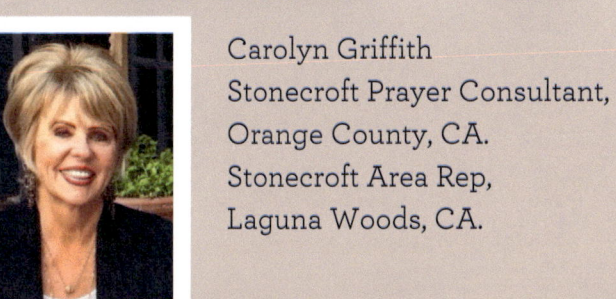

Carolyn Griffith
Stonecroft Prayer Consultant,
Orange County, CA.
Stonecroft Area Rep,
Laguna Woods, CA.

"For I am about to do

something new.

See, I have already begun!
Do you not see it? I will
make a pathway through the
wilderness. I will create
rivers in the dry wasteland."

Isaiah 43:19 NLT

Made in the USA
Columbia, SC
25 April 2024

34698339R00035